CW00517276

SEEING INTO THE UNSEEN REALM

Vivianne Duah-Odei

~ ABOUT THE AUTHOR ~

Vivianne is a radio presenter for Girl Talk; a ministry for females of all ages and Hour of Encounter on Elim Radio UK. She is a teacher of the Word and is deeply passionate about the things of God.

Vivianne has the desire to see individuals, communities, nations and governments transformed by the power of God. She loves evangelizing and has a passion for seeing souls won for Jesus Christ. Vivianne has been fascinated by the Word of God and has occasionally allowed her unique access into the spiritual realm.

~ ABOUT DIVINE ENCOUNTER ~

In this exciting and revelatory book, the Author has chronicled every extraordinary encounter she experienced with the Lord. Vivianne describes her incredible journey, explaining how God opened her spiritual eyes to bear witness to the realm that our natural eyes do not see.

The Author's story will move you into the realm of intercession; it will empower you to reach out to tell people how real God is and how much He loved us and sacrificed his only begotten Son for us all.

~ DISCLAIMER ~

The visions mentioned in this book are not introduced to worship angels, but to recognize that they are contributing ministers.

They are here to help us fulfil our assignment on earth. The task God has given us requires practical and spiritual helpers.

As Christians, we need to partner with God to reach our final destination and hear Him say: *"Well done my good and faithful servant."*

DIVINE ENCOUNTER

Seeing into the Unseen Realm

ISBN: 9798668417582

~ DEDICATION ~

I dedicate this book to God the Father, God the Son, God the Holy Spirit, who are my inspiration for writing this book. I also dedicate this book to my husband Adams and four beautiful children.

My handsome Jeremiah who God uses to speak to me most of the time, my beautiful princess Nesiah who loves worshipping God all the time and my angel Eliana who makes everyone laugh,to my brave son Kwame who is always up for a challenge. You are all indeed a gift sent from God, and I love you all very much.

~ ACKNOWLEDGEMENTS ~

Thank you to Dr Morris Cerullo, whose prayers activated my spiritual senses.

To Reverend Kwesi Adzam and First Lady Mrs Adjoa Adzam; thank you for all your support and encouragement throughout the years.

A big thank you to Mr Emmanuel Fabin for his contribution to this book. May God richly bless you and increase you more and more.

Prophet Seth Tetteh; thank you for all your prayers and encouragement throughout the years.

TABLE OF CONTENTS

About The Author   ii
About Divine Encounter   iii
Disclaimer   iv
Dedication   vi
Acknowledgements   vii
Introduction   1
What Is The Purpose Of A Divine Encounter?   3
Spiritual Doors, Windows, Paths,Time and Seasons   15
Ranks of Angels   26
Types of Angels   30
Angels and Ministers   36
Characteristic of Angels   42
Angels and the End Times   46
Salvation   48
The Power of Opened Eyes   50
I Feel Safe   55
Anymore and I will Explode   56
And the Heavens were Opened   59
The Holy Spirit   63
The King of Kings - Jesus Christ of Nazareth   71
THE KING OF GLORY   74
The Servant King   80
An appointment with Almighty God   84
The Ultimate Royal Family   94
How to activate your spiritual senses   105
Activation Prayer   122
BIBLIOGRAPHY   124

~ INTRODUCTION ~

What is a Divine Encounter?
A divine encounter comes with a profound revelation of hidden secrets. Divine means that which emanates from God.

Encounter means to meet face-to-face suddenly or unexpectedly.

A divine encounter can change the trajectory of one's life. Take Saul of Tarsus for example; he believed in God and thought he was helping God by persecuting anyone who believed in Jesus as the Messiah.

One day, something happened to Saul. While on his way to Damascus, a bright light suddenly appeared from heaven which blinded Saul on the spot. He fell to the ground and heard a voice saying unto him, "Saul, Saul! Why are you persecuting me?" Saul replied, "Who are you, Lord?" And the Lord said, "I am Jesus whom you are persecuting."

Saul could not remain the same. The encounter changed his name, his nature and his destiny forever.

He went on to become one of the greatest Apostles in contributing to the New Testament. He went from being a persecutor of the church to becoming one of the greatest Bible teachers to add to the New Testament and win the Gentiles to Christ in just one divine encounter.

I have come to an understanding that life is not just physical; it is also supernatural. The supernatural element is needed to make all the difference and determine the direction of your life. You need to encounter God and experience the reality of Christ. The death, burial and resurrection of Jesus is not a myth; it is the power of God unto Salvation.

~ CHAPTER 1 ~

WHAT IS THE PURPOSE OF A DIVINE ENCOUNTER?

Colossians 1:16 says: "For by Him were all things created, that are in Heaven, and that are in earth, physical and spiritual realm, whether [they be] thrones, or dominions, or principalities, or powers: He created all things through Him and for Him."

Colossians 1:16(NIV)

A divine encounter helps to anchor our faith and belief in God. It does not mean that you shouldn't believe in God. If you have not experienced a divine visitation or an encounter yet, do not be discouraged. Jesus said to Thomas "Blessed are those who have not seen, but yet believe."

However, with that said, having a personal encounter builds confidence within you; when things get difficult in your life, you can pinpoint where you had an encounter with God, as it gives an assurance that God has not forgotten about you, and will always be present regardless of the circumstances.

A perfect example in the Bible is Jacob who raised an altar at Bethel; this means *the house of God*. He said, "God was here and I did not know it!"

In the book of Genesis 28:11-13 NIV, we read about Jacob's ladder: (11) He came to a certain place and spent the night there because the sun had set, and he took one of the stones of the place and put it under his head and laid down. (12) He had a dream, and behold, a ladder was set on the earth with its top reaching to heaven, and behold, and the angels of God were ascending and descending on it. (13) And behold, the Lord stood above it and said, "I am the LORD, the God of your father Abraham and the God of Isaac; the land on which you lie, I will give it to you and your descendant."

The significance of the encounter Jacob experienced was being able to see the angels on the ladder. Up until that point, no one knew there was a staircase touching between earth and heaven. The angels ascending was taking prayer requests up to God and the ones descending were coming down with answers to prayers for the saints.

An angel of the Lord engaged Jacob in a conversation regarding his identity. The angel asked him for his name to which he replied *Jacob*. The angel replied: "Your name is not Jacob, but your name is Israel". Jacob means *trickster* but now, Israel, his new name means *a prince of God*.

The dialogue between the angel and Jacob helps me to know that our real identity is not based on the name our biological parents gave us but is predicated on what God has written concerning us.

As King David proclaimed in the Old Testament in Psalm 40:7: Then I said, "Behold, I come; in the scroll of the book it is written of me. We see King Jesus in the New Testament proclaiming the same thing in Hebrews 10:7:
Then I said, "Here I am, it is written about me in the scroll; I have come to do your will, my God".

The Father validates who He is at the Jordan River on the mountain of transfiguration.

"So, beloved do not allow people to define you by what you are currently facing, but let God reveal who you are based on what He has written concerning your life."

"For I know the plans I have for you declares the LORD, plans to prosper you and not to harm you, plans to give you hope and a future." Jeremiah 29:11 (NIV)

In the new testament, we read in the book of John 1:29-34 that Jesus had an encounter with the Holy Spirit during His baptism in the River Jordan and soon after the Holy Spirit led Him into the wilderness; Jesus fasted for forty days and overcame Satan's temptations.

I have come to discover that in life, we cannot experience promotion without the help of God. If Jesus Christ who is the King of Kings needed the assistance of the supernatural, then why not us? We see instances in the Bible where angels released strength to him in reference to Luke 22:42-43.

In the book of Matthew 2:13, an angel of the Lord appeared to Joseph in a dream to identify what steps to take in saving the life of his Son, Jesus. They had escaped to Egypt to hide from King Herod who plotted to kill all male Jewish babies as a threat to terminate Jesus.

I find it strange that during the time of Moses' birth, Pharaoh was killing all male babies during the birth of Jesus.
However, Joseph and Mary had to escape to Egypt by divine instruction; a place where the Israelites were once afflicted and oppressed for so long, yet baby Jesus found safety there.

That is why these divine encounters are critical and imperative. You never know where your deliverance or provision will come from; only God knows.

When He gives you an instruction through a divine encounter, it might not make sense the moment you receive it, but as you are obedient and follow His instructions you realise it will make sense in the end.

Sometimes, people have divine encounters because they have the gift to see into the supernatural. In Matthew 13:16 it reads: "But blessed are your eyes because they see, and your ears because they hear."

The Holy Spirit is the one who knows the heart of the Father and searches the deep things of God. In other words, we need to allow the Holy Spirit to teach and guide us.

It is written in 1 Corinthians 2:9: "What no eye has seen, what no ear has heard and what no human mind has conceived the things God has prepared for those who love Him." These are the things God has revealed to us by His Spirit.

The Bible is full of many examples of God revealing Himself to people unexpectedly. These encounters often resulted in changing the trajectory of people's lives.

God explained to the people of Israel why He allowed them to have such encounters. This is in Deuteronomy 4:35 which says: "You were shown these things so that you might know that the Lord is God; besides Him, there is no other."

We live in a parallel world; when you wake up from bed, you wake up to two worlds in motion.

We live in the physical and the spiritual realm; not just the natural realm that a lot of people view as being all there is. *I have come to discover that the spiritual realm is more real than the natural realm.* The *physical realm* is *temporary*, and the *spiritual realm* is *eternal*. In fact, whatever happens in the natural realm takes place in the spiritual realm; before it manifests itself in the physical.

Have you ever had a dream, and days after, you begin to see what you saw in the dream taking place right before your eyes? Well, it has happened to me several times. Most of the time, if I do not like what I saw in the dream, I'd pray for God to cancel it and replace it with something good by declaring the blessings of God before it transitions into the natural realm.

In the book of Revelation, it says Jesus was crucified before the foundation of the world. Revelation 13:8 clarifies that all inhabitants of the earth will worship the beast; all whose names have not been written in the book of life belonging to the Lamb that was slain from the creation of the world.

This means the crucifixion of Christ Jesus took place in the realm of the spirit before it took place in the natural realm. Understanding how the spiritual realm operates is fundamental to our walk with God.

In the spiritual realm, there are times and seasons, doors, portals, windows, paths, highways and much more.

When I discovered that I could see into the realm of the spirit, I was so excited, but my dilemma was who can I share these visions and dreams with, until I discovered a show called: *"It's supernatural"* presented by Sid Roth.

I could not contain my excitement, especially when I heard the guests of the show talking about the visions God had shown them, and most of them were like what I have seen.

Eventually, it became my favourite show. I would watch it day and night to the point I felt empowered to share my vision without feeling weird or awkward.

Hence, why I have chosen to write this book. Believe me, it was not an easy decision. I remember while I was waiting for confirmation from God before writing, I had a dream. I found myself in Liberia and was talking to a woman and was telling her about one of the encounters I had with the Lord. After I finished speaking, the woman was shocked and said she wanted to give her life to Christ.

When I woke up, I decided not to take these dreams for granted but rather use it as an evangelical tool.

Exercising your spiritual senses

You can be in church for years and not know God; *you cannot know God with your physical senses; you can only know Him through your spiritual senses.*

How do you activate your spiritual senses?

You activate your spiritual senses by excising it through the tests and storms of life. Although we do not like trials and storms, that is the only way we can develop our spiritual senses.

Our faith is a test; we are given a measure of faith and will depend on your reason for using it effectively.

The same way you develop physical senses are similar to how you develop spiritual senses. Take it like this; the trials of life are like a gymnasium; Faith, Fasting, Prayer, the Word, Praise & Worship are the several gym equipments. Exercise: The Greek word for exercise is *gymnasia* which

means "to train, workout, and exercise" and the root of the English term, "*gymnasium*" – means physical training (bodily exercise).

1   Timothy 4:8 refers to physical disciplines - Imagine two men with muscles; one has developed his. He now looks like a bodybuilder and the other person has not developed his muscles yet, he looks slimmer. Nonetheless, he has the same muscles as the other man.

The only difference is that one has developed his muscles, and the other one hasn't. The reason why many people don't develop their spiritual senses is they react to everything with their natural feelings.

The Bible says: "He who has an ear let him hear what the spirit is saying". What does this piece of scripture mean? Specifically, everyone who has an ear, let him listen to what is being said.

We all have ears, although this verse isn't referring to our natural ears, but referring to our inner man, just as we have ears to hear sounds in the natural, we have an inner ear to listen to what the spirit of the Lord is saying.

Hebrews 5:11-14 says: "We have much to say about this, but it is hard to explain because you are dull of hearing.

(12) Although by this time you ought to be teachers, you need someone to reteach you the basic principles of God's word. You need milk, not solid food. (13) Everyone who lives on milk is still an infant, inexperienced in the message of righteousness. (14) But solid food is for the mature, who by constant use have trained their sensibilities to distinguish good from evil."

We also have spiritual eyes, just as the natural eyes help us see in the physical realm, our spiritual eyes help us to see in the spiritual realm.

2   Kings 6:15-17 NIV says: "(15) When the servant of the man of God got up and went out early the next morning, an army with horses and chariots had surrounded the city. Oh no, my Lord! What shall we do?" the servant asked. (16) 'Don't be afraid', the prophet answered. 'Those who are with us are more than those who are with them', (17) And Elisha prayed, 'Open his eyes, Lord, so that he may see'. Then the Lord opened the servant's eyes, and he looked and saw the hills full of horses and chariots of fire all around Elisha."

This verse lets me know that Elisha's servant had spiritual eyes, but he just was not using it properly.

In order to defeat the enemy, you need all your spiritual senses activated. That is how you can know where the enemy is attacking you from. When you work out your spiritual senses you get the heavenly hosts to act in your defense; that is why the enemy tries to get you to operate in the flesh all the time.

In Hebrews 4:7-10 it reads: "During the days of Jesus' earthly life, He offered up prayers and petitions with loud cries and tears to the One who could save him from death; and He was heard because of His reverence. (8) Although He was a Son, He learned obedience from what He suffered. (9) And having been made perfect, He became the source of eternal salvation to all who obey Him. (10) and was designated by God as high priest in the order of Melchizedek.

Fasting

Fasting is one way of activating your spiritual senses. Fasting is a spiritual discipline; denying your flesh and pleasures. Your spiritual faculties are then tuned to the frequency of heaven which makes it easier to pick up spiritual things.

The following are examples of the various ways to fast:

-      You can deny yourself food.
-      You can fast from television and social media.

Praying in the Spirit

Praying in the Spirit helps to build yourself in your most Holy Faith. If you do not exercise your spiritual senses, they become dull, and you remain a spiritual baby. You might be a Christian for a long period of time, but in the realm of the Spirit, you may not have a clue when it comes to spiritual things.

~CHAPTER 2~

SPIRITUAL DOORS, WINDOWS, PATHS, TIME AND SEASONS

(11) Then an angel of the Lord appeared to him, standing on the right side of the altar of incense. (12) And when Zacharias saw him, he was troubled, and fear fell upon him.
(13) But the angel said to him, "Do not be afraid, Zacharias, for your prayer is heard and your wife Elizabeth will bear you a son, and you shall call his name John."
Luke 1:11-13 (NIV)

In the spiritual realm, there are times and seasons, doors, portals, windows, paths, highways and much more.

What is a Spiritual Window?

Malachi 3:10 is a scripture we should know very well; it tells us to: "bring all the tithes into the storehouse so there will be enough food in my temple. If you do, says the Lord of Heavens Armies, I will open the windows of heaven for you. I will pour out a blessing so great you would not have enough room to take it in! Try it! Put me to the test."

I am sure you have heard the term: "window of opportunity". In order words, change can be referred to windows.

I firmly believe every good opportunity we get is from Almighty God. I once heard a preacher say when you pay your tithes, stop looking for money; instead look for ideas. God can easily drop ideas in your mind. If you implement this plan, it can potentially earn you millions.

I heard a story where a hairdresser took notice of what her preacher said, to pay close attention to the ideas received, because it could be a God-given idea. She went home thinking of how she would come up with a hair product line or an appliance that will revolutionise the hairdressing industry.

However, that night before she went to bed, God had better ideas. God planted a diagram in her dream so when the lady woke up, she said to herself' "what kind of layout is this?" Immediately, she decided to draw a picture she saw and research about the diagram. News broke out about her design.

It turned out a medical research company heard about her diagram and they gave her a call. She went to the laboratory and showed them the layout; it was a scientific diagram. This would give the medical researchers the breakthrough they desperately needed.

The head of the department decided to offer the lady $20 million dollars to take ownership of the diagram. The lady was asked if she would accept the offer of $20 million dollars and if that was too small they would be prepared to increase it. Trembling and in total shock with the amount she heard, she accepted the $20 million dollars.

Ladies and gentlemen, this is what God can do. One idea can change the course of your life. That is a spiritual window or what we call a *"window of opportunity"*.

Open Doors
Revelation 3:7-8 (NIV): "And to the angel of the church in Philadelphia wrote: He who is holy, who is true, who has the key of David, who opens, and no one will shut, and who shuts, and no one opens".

What is an open door? An open door is a means of admission or access.

The verse we read in Revelation 3:7-8 says that God has the key to life and when He gives you access to an opportunity, no one can deny you the favour God has given. That is why when you end up in the place of influence or success.

People around you may wonder how you got there. It is because God gave you access to an open door that no man can shut. *If a man gives you access to an open door, they will take credit for it* but if God gives you an opportunity, all the Glory belongs to Him.

If God says He doesn't want you to have something, it doesn't matter how much you force yourself to have it; you are wasting time because what He says is final. If you decide you do not want it God's way, it would not be a pleasant experience. Ladies and gentlemen let us pray for the grace to do things God's way. It is the sure way of which you are going to experience total victory.

Highways
Isaiah 35:8 says: "A highway will be there, a roadway, and it will be called the Highway of Holiness. The unclean will not travel on it, but it will be for him who walks that way, and fools will not wander on it."

Jesus had to be born during the time of the Roman Empire since they were the only empire who colonised people but left them in their own country. To manage all the people, they had subjugated, they created highways and roads to connect the towns and cities to give them access to the different countries.

The Roman Empire was very advanced in their thinking; however, what they did not know was they were setting up everything in place to welcome the Saviour of the world.

That is why I am not surprised when John the Baptist said: *a highway or roadway would be there.*

The constructed roads meant Jesus could travel from city to city preaching about the Kingdom. They will be the only empire whose capital punishment would be by crucifixion.

He had to shed His blood without breaking any of his bones in the process. That was the plan at least, as Roman centurions were obliged to break criminals' bones after they died.

However, when Christ died on the cross and a Roman centurion wanted to break His legs, God intervened and stopped him. There was a limit as to how far they could go.

Jesus could not have died by execution or an electric chair hence why He came during the Roman Empire. You might be going through unpleasant situations at this moment in time, but I believe God will use it as a highway to connect the dots and life will finally make sense.

You will look back in the years to come and say like Job: "My suffering was good for me, for it taught me to pay attention to Your decrees."

Spiritual Path
A spiritual path is what God lays out for us. If we follow the path, we will not only fulfil our purpose in life, we will reach our final destination.

Psalms 16:11 says: "You make known to me the path of life; you will fill me with joy in your presence, with eternal pleasures at your right hand."

Proverbs 4:18 (NIV) says: "The path of the righteous is like the morning sun, shining ever brighter till the full light of day."

Dreams
Job 33-15:17: says: "(15) In a dream, a vision of the night, when sound sleep falls on men. While they slumber in their beds. (16) Then He opens the ears of men and seals their instruction. (17) He may turn man aside from his conduct and keep a man from pride."

Another way God speaks to me is through dreams. I make sure I don't indulge in unedifying programmes before going to bed because I don't want such things to influence my dream negatively.

When I go to bed after prayers, my dreams are clearer and sharper. Although there are other ways God speaks to me.

At times, it is through the written word of God that gives me a *Rhema word* which is the Holy Spirit bringing the scriptures to life.

Another way the Lord speaks to us is through a still small voice; when the Holy Spirit is communicating with us, sometimes it can be the audible voice of God. He can also speak to us through his servants through authentic, credible men and women of God.
How do you know, whether what you are seeing or hearing is from God?

First, you have an inner peace about it and will always align with the word of God.

Another way is being in a state of trance:

What is a trance?

1.   A half-conscious state, seemingly between sleeping and waking, in which ability to function voluntarily may be suspended.

2.   A dazed or bewildered condition.

The Bible says that both Paul and Peter fell into a trance. According to the book of Acts 10:9-16:

"(9)   The next day at about the sixth hour, as the men were approaching the city on their journey, Peter went up on the roof to pray.

(10)   He became hungry and wanted something to eat, but while the meal was being prepared, he fell into a trance.

(11)   He saw heaven open and something like a large sheet being let down to earth by its four corners.

(12)   It contained all kinds of four-footed animals and reptiles of the earth, as well as birds of the air.

(13)   Then a voice spoke to him saying: "get up, Peter, kill and eat!"

(14)   "No, Lord!" Peter answered, "I have never eaten anything impure or unclean."

(15)   The voice spoke to him a second time: "Do not call anything impure that God has made clean."

(16)   This happened three times, and all at once the sheet was taken back up into heaven. This encounter was the beginning of the Gentiles being engrafted in the salvation plan, or should I say the revealing of God's plans for the Gentiles.

Due to this divine encounter, Peter discovered God's sovereignty, which was to include the Gentiles in the redemption plan. In other words, Christ did not die for the Jews only, as Peter thought initially. Since Peter was the head of the church, God was letting Peter in on the plan, and he was to be the initiator of the project by introducing the Gentiles to the Gospel of Christ.

While Peter was puzzled over the meaning of the vision, the men sent by Cornelius found Simon's house and approached the gate. They called out to ask if Simon called Peter,and if he was living there. As Peter continued to reflect on the vision, the Spirit told him, "Three men are here looking for you. Get up! Go downstairs and accompany them without hesitation, because I have sent them."

Peter went down to the men and said, "Here am I, the one you are looking for, Why have you come?" "Cornelius, the centurion, has sent us," they said. "He is a righteous and God-fearing man with a good reputation among the whole Jewish nation.

A holy angel instructed him to request your presence in his home so that he could hear a message from you." So Peter invited them in as his guests. And the next day he got ready and went with them, accompanied by some of the brothers from Joppa. The Gentiles Receive the Holy Spirit.

Times and Seasons

I can safely say times have changed. What do you mean by that? Let me explain, history let us know that we have moved from the agricultural age to the industrial age and we are now in the information age. As it is in the natural, so it is in the spiritual.

We are living in the last days; the things that are happening all around us indicates we are closer to the return of Christ than we think. In the first return of Christ, He came as a Lamb. He was a meek saviour but this time He is not coming as a Lamb, He is coming as a Lion.

He is not going to be beaten, stripped and crucified as was the case in His first coming. He is returning as a bold King. My question is, are we preparing to meet Him?

1 Chronicles 12:32 says: "Of the children of Issachar, men who understood the times, to know what Israel ought to do, their heads were two hundred; and all their brothers were at their commandment.

Beloved it's important to understand the times and seasons in which we live, and even though we need to keep up to date with the economy, politics and much more, it is imperative that we stay grounded in our sound biblical principle". Otherwise, we can be carried away by any wave of doctrine.

RANKS OF ANGELS

*Then I heard the angel in charge of the water saying righteous
art thou,who art and who wast,thou Holy One, because thou
Holy One, because thou didst thus judge:*
Revelation 16:5 (ASV)

The Bible lets us know that there are levels about the
creation of God. For example, the lion is the head of the
beast. Human beings are the zenith of all creation and in
the same way, a C.E.O is the director of a corporation.

As it is in the natural, so it is in the spiritual. The angelic
realm is in rank and order; the highest ranking is the
archangel.

The word archangel is mentioned two times in the Bible
in reference to 1 Thessalonian 4:16-17 which reads: "(16)
For the Lord, Himself will come down from Heaven,
with a loud command, with the voice of the archangel
and with the trumpet call of God, and the dead in Christ
will rise first. (17) After that, we who are still alive and
are left will be caught up together with them in the
clouds to meet the Lord in the air. And so, we will be
with the Lord forever."

For the Lord, Himself will descend from Heaven with a shout, with the voice of an archangel and with the trumpet of God.

But even the archangel Michael, when he was disputing with the devil about the body of Moses, did not himself dare to condemn him for slander but said, "The Lord rebuke you!"

Michael and Gabriel are the only angels whom the Bible calls an archangel. The name Michael means "who is like our God".

Angel Michael is also known as the celestial prince of Israel and the commander in chief over the army of the living God also known as the Host of Heaven.

The Book of Daniel
Daniel 10:12-14 (KJV) says: "(12) Then he continued, "Do not be afraid, Daniel. Since the first day that you set your mind to gain understanding and to humble yourself before your God, your words were heard, and I have come in response to them.

(13) But the prince of the Persian kingdom resisted me for twenty-one days. Then Michael, one of the chief princes came to help me because I was detained there with the king of Persia. (14) Now I have come to explain to you what will happen to your people in the future, for the vision concerns a time yet to come."

It revealed how Michael was called to assist a lower ranking angel to help defeat the prince of Persia, while on his way to deliver answers to Daniel's prayer.

In the book of Revelation, God refuses to fight with his creation, Lucifer. God left the war that broke out in heaven into the capable hands of Archangel Michael. Revelation 12:7-9 (NIV) states: "(7) Then war broke out in Heaven. Michael and his angels fought against the dragon, and the dragon and his angels fought back. (8) But he was not strong enough and lost their place in heaven. (9) The great dragon was hurled down — that ancient serpent called the devil, or Satan, who leads the whole world astray. He was thrown to the earth and his angels with him."

What I like personally about angels is they follow God's instruction to the letter; they are always obedient to God.

The second archangel mentioned in the bible is angel Gabriel. Gabriel means; man of God. He is responsible for delivering messages. He is also a high-ranking angel due to the type of messages he brings.

He emphasized his ranking by revealing to Zacharias who he was, and I quote "I am Gabriel who stands in the very presence of God". In other words, he was saying, my words carry power and therefore I am not a low-ranking angel.

Beginning from the book of Daniel in the old testament. Daniel 9:20-23 (NIV) in reference to the seventy "sevens", the scripture reads: "(20) While I was speaking and praying, confessing my sin, the sins of my people Israel and making my request to the Lord my God for his holy hill. (21). While I was still in prayer, Gabriel, the man I had seen in the earlier vision, came to me in swift flight about the time of the evening sacrifice. (22) He instructed me and said, 'Daniel, I have now come to give you insight and understanding. (23) As soon as you began to pray, a word went out, which I have come to tell you, for you are highly esteemed. Therefore, consider the word and understand the vision.'"

~ CHAPTER 4 ~

TYPES OF ANGELS

Cherubim and Seraphim

Above him stood the seraphim. Each had six wings: with two he covered his face, and with two he covered his feet, and with two he flew.

Isaiah 6:2 (ESV)

These types of angels were first mentioned in the book of Genesis 3:24. Cherubim and seraphim are very close to the throne of God as stated in the book of 1 Samuel 4:4.

Ezekiel 10:1-21 reads:
"(1) I looked, and I saw the likeness of a throne of lapis lazuli above the vault that was over the heads of the cherubim.

(2)   The LORD said to the man clothed in linen, "Go in among the wheels beneath the cherubim. Fill your hands with burning coals from among the cherubim and scatter them over the city." And as I watched, he went in.

(3)   Now the cherubim were standing on the south side of the temple when the man went in, and a cloud filled the inner court.

(4)   Then the glory of the LORD rose from above the cherubim and moved to the threshold of the temple. The cloud filled the temple, and the court was full of the radiance of the glory of the LORD.

(5)   The sound of the wings of the cherubim could be heard as far away as the outer court, like the voice of God Almighty when he speaks.

(6)   When the LORD commanded the man in linen, "Take fire from among the wheels, from among the cherubim," the man went in and stood beside a wheel.

(7)   Then one of the cherubim reached out his hand to the fire that was among them. He took up some of it and put it into the hands of the man in linen, who took it and went out.

(8)   Under the wings of the cherubim could be seen what looked like human hands.

(9)   I looked, and I saw beside the cherubim four wheels, one beside each of the cherubim; the wheels sparkled like topaz.

(10)   As for their appearance, the four of them looked alike; each was like a wheel intersecting a wheel.

(11) As they moved, they would go in any one of the four directions the cherubim faced; the wheels did not turn about as the cherubim went. The cherubim went in whatever direction the head faced, without turning as they went.

(12) Their entire bodies, including their backs, their hands, and their wings, were full of eyes, as were their four wheels.

(13) I heard the wheels being called "the whirling wheels."

(14) Each of the cherubim had four faces: One face was that of a cherub, the second the face of a human being, the third the face of a lion, and the fourth the face of an eagle.

(15) Then the cherubim rose upward. These were the living creatures I had seen by the Kebar River.

(16) When the cherubim moved, the wheels beside them moved; and when the cherubim spread their wings to rise from the ground, the wheels did not leave their side.

(17) When the cherubim stood still, they also stood still; and when the cherubim rose, they rose with them, because the spirit of the living creatures was in them.

(18) Then the glory of the LORD departed from over the threshold of the temple and stopped above the cherubim.

(19) While I watched, the cherubim spread their wings and rose from the ground, and as they went, the wheels went with them. They stopped at the entrance of the east gate of the LORD's house, and the glory of the God of Israel was above them.

(20) These were the living creatures I had seen beneath the God of Israel by the Kebar River, and I realized that they were cherubim.

(21) Each had four faces and four wings, and under their wings was what looked like human hands."

Ezekiel described what the cherubim looked like and what they could do.

Seraphim
Seraphim is mention in the book of Isaiah 6:1-4 which reads:

"(1) In the year that King Uzziah died, I saw the Lord, high and exalted, seated on a throne; and the train of his robe filled the temple.

(2) Above him were seraphim, each with six wings: With two wings they covered their faces, with two they covered their feet, and with two they were flying.

(3) And they were calling to one another: "Holy, holy, holy is the Lord Almighty; The whole earth is full of his glory."

(4) At the sound of their voices, the doorposts and thresholds shook, and the temple was filled with smoke."
Seraphim means burning or fiery
Isaiah 6:5-7 (NIV) reads: "(5). "Woe to me!" I cried. "I am ruined! For I am a man of unclean lips, and I live among a people of unclean lips, and my eyes have seen the King, the Lord Almighty." (6). Then one of the seraphim flew to me with a live coal in his hand, which he had taken with tongs from the altar. (7) With it, he touched my mouth and said, "See, this has touched your lips; your guilt is taken away, and your sin atoned for."

Personally, I had encounters with angels who poured "fire" on me every time I finished praying at night. For some reason, they always wait for me to fall asleep before they start their work.

If I didn't sleep straight away and decided to go on my phone browsing on social media, they would wait. If it was getting to day break and I'm still on my phone, the angels would have done something for me to sleep.

This reminds me of when an angel wanted to leave before day break, but Jacob would not allow him in reference to Genesis 32:25-27 (NIV):

"(25) When the man saw that he could not overpower him, he touched the socket of Jacob's hip so that his hip was stretched as he wrestled with the man. (26) Then the man said, "Let me go, for it is daybreak." But Jacob replied, "I will not let you go unless you bless me." (27) The man asked him, "What is your name?" "Jacob," he answered."

So far, God allowed me to see two types of angels:
1)   Angels with wings and the ones without
2)   Angels who look like humans

ANGELS AND MINISTERS

*Micaiah continued, 'Therefore hear the word of the LORD: I
saw the LORD sitting on his throne with all the multitudes of
heaven standing around him on his right and his left.*
King 22:19(NIV)

The Lord has occasionally allowed me to see angels and
ministers of God, especially when they are ministering.
I have seen angels of God ministering alongside
preachers and prophets; they go wherever the minister
goes.

They are usually on the left and the right. There was a
time I saw four angels around one minister; two on the
left and two on the right; it was a quick flash. I remember
moving back in awe.

The type of angels sent to assist ministers and preachers
in ministry depended on the spiritual ranking of the
minister and the level of anointing or influence they
have.

I am referring to a true man of God, not false prophets. I
have seen great men of God who are well known; the
angels were taller and had powerful wings.

I remember going to a leadership conference and the time came for those who would like to have the spirit of leadership come forward to receive prayers. I went to the altar along with others.

While I was waiting for my turn, people around me were falling under the power of God. As the man of God walked past me, I felt a strong presence that I nearly passed out to be honest with you.

I tried to gain consciousness and immediately asked God what that was! He opened my spiritual eyes to the angel next to the right side of the Bishop.

I was shocked when I saw him and was taken back. I realised it was the weight of glory the angel was carrying that nearly made me pass out. Note: high ranking angels are more powerful. Due to this powerful man of God being well known, his warfare is more different compared to other ministers in local churches.

I also believe highly anointed men or women of God have high ranking angels to equip and empower them in ministry.

During church service, spiritual activities are at its highest, which is the time to be sensitive to the Holy Spirit and know what God is doing. God lives in us through his Spirit, and we are aware of this, but there are times when his manifested presence fills the room especially during praise and worship, and the whole atmosphere changes from ordinary to extraordinary.

There are times when during worship, I have opened my eyes, and could see a thick cloud of fog covering above the heads of the entire congregation. I tried putting my hand through it and my hand will shake uncontrollably. I smiled and said God is here!

Have you ever been in a church service where you were basking in the presence of God, and you suddenly realised God was there? That is your spiritual senses at work.

During church services, I would expect the whole atmosphere to change; I am not standing there passively but heavily engaged with the worship experience. Trying to discern when the atmosphere changes or shifts, the moment the presence of God arrives, I feel Him in my spirit.

Most of the time I feel like running across the altar, why? Because when He arrives, His presence brings liberty. Yokes are broken, depression vacates, demons flee, because that is what the power of God can do.

I remember a time when I felt liberated in my spirit when the presence of God came down and wanted to run across the stage. I knew people would not understand, but then a time came that I could not contain my excitement.

There came a time in my life where I just stopped caring about what people thought of me. I ran across the stage because I felt so liberated in my spirit with my new-found freedom. I tried going back to my seat, but I couldn't!

The only way to describe the power of God was like a rushing wind blowing you to the opposite direction. The current was pushing me back to stay where I was, except this was spiritual wind with fire from God; it was awesome! I had to hold on the railings to keep me upright.

I found out through a dream a huge angel was standing in front of my church pulpit, so I wanted to know if what I saw in my dream was true. The following Sunday, I deliberately danced near the pulpit where he was standing. To my amazement, not only was the angel there, but he was releasing the power of God to everyone who went past him.

Each time I reached that spot, I felt my strength being renewed. During one of our church services, my pastor was preaching and began declaring blessing on us. He started walking down the aisle, when God opened my spiritual eyes.

I saw two glorious angels; one on his left and one on his right. The words that were coming out of his mouth felt like lighting. I am saying all of this so you pay close attention when you go to church and not to be distracted by what others are doing.

One thing about the supernatural is that once you are exposed to it, you become a student of that realm. When you experience God, it is an introduction to what you are entitled to, through the shedding blood of our Lord and Saviour Jesus Christ.

God does not take us into such experiences to tease us about what is going to happen in eternity. He allows us into that realm where we must steward to come into it more often.

Having divine encounters does not necessarily bring you a renewed mind; you need to be a student of the Word as that is what brings about a new sense of renewal.

Divine encounters give you the confidence that God is *real.*

~ C H A P T E R 6 ~

CHARACTERISTIC OF ANGELS

But even the archangel Michael, when he was disputing with the devil about the body of Moses, did not himself dare to condemn him for slander but said, 'The Lord rebuke you!''
Jude 1:9(NIV)

Angels are brilliant creatures; we see all throughout the bible their ability to quote scriptures. Angels have a free will.

They have a choice whether to obey God or not. Angels are ministering spirits. We see their strength and how powerful they are. I do not believe they are omniscient or omnipotent; only Almighty God is.

Ephesian 3:10 makes a statement which says some mysteries are hidden from the angels, and they can only unlock those secrets by watching us; the church in action. Whenever we relate to God as a church, the angels are taking notes trying to gain an understanding regarding the mystery of the Gospel.

Ephesians 3:10-11 reads: "(10) His purpose was that now, through the church, the manifold wisdom of God should be made known to the rulers and authorities in the heavenly realms. (11) According to the eternal purpose that He accomplished in Christ Jesus our Lord."

What is it about humanity that God can't get us out of his mind? We are made from dust' we break God's law all the time, we walk out of order, and *we are mostly interested in our agenda instead of God's agenda*. He sends His only begotten Son to shed His blood for us on the cross of Calvary.

That is why the angel asked God: "What is man that thou art mindful of the Son of Man that thou visited."

Angels and Worship
Some angels join us in worshiping our creator. If we kneel during worship, they also kneel; if we lift our hands, they will lift their hands. If we lay prostrate on the floor in awe of our Maker, the angels would do the same. Their main task is to worship God with us.

Angels and Prayer
This is also known as 'warfare angels'. These angels come down to battle with us during prayer or spiritual warfare. I remember a time I was dwelling on my intentions in serving God faithfully but did not see any significant change in my life.

I took matters into my own hands and decided to have my all-night vigil to see if there would be an improvement in my life.

I put my quilt on the living room floor and would sleep and wake up at 12:00am and pray till 6:00am. My prayer plan was to speak in tongues for at least an hour and pray for three hours, worshipping, and ending with studying the bible .

I kept doing this until the third day came. I noticed things were shifting in the realm of the spirit. I'd sense the Holy Spirit driving out unclean spirits in my house. He said that financial difficulties should go! Even though I was sleeping, I could see what was going on in the spiritual realm.

I saw demons as tall as my door running in a hurry to get out of my house. I could see them struggling to get out and were stuck at the door. The Holy Spirit knew where they were hiding so when I started the night vigil, the house became too hot for them to stay.

The following day before 12:00am, I had a quick vision. This was the vision of mighty warrior angels with massive wings flying from heaven towards me. The vision ended just after that. I quickly got up with so much joy and enthusiasm ready to pray. I mean if all these warrior angels are here to back me up in prayer, what I am waiting for! It's time to fire some prayers.

After that my life changed dramatically. I went from living a stagnant life to having my ministry. Every Saturday I have the privilege of ministering to young women across the world through a radio station called Elim Radio UK. My Show is called Girl TALK. Yes, you heard right, I went from being a "nobody" to having influence; that is what God can do.

When we seek Him with all our hearts, we will find Him.

ANGELS AND THE END TIMES

TheThen another angel, who had power to destroy with fire, came from the altar. He shouted to the angel with the sharp sickle, ''Swing your sickle now to gather the cluster of grapes from the vines the earth, for they are ripe for judgement.''
Revelation 14:18(NLT)

The Angels will assist the Lord at the end times. They have been prepared for it and will be in their posts when the trumpet sounds. They will be doing what they have been instructed to do.

Matthew 13:37-43 reads:
"(37) He answered, "The one who sowed the good seed is the Son of Man.

(38)   The field is the world, and the good seed stands for the people of the kingdom. The weeds are the people of the evil one.

(39)   And the enemy who sows them is the devil. The harvest is the end of the age, and the harvesters are angels.

(40)   "As the weeds are pulled up and burned in the fire so that it will be at the end of the age.

(41) The Son of Man will send out his angels, and they will weed out of his kingdom everything that causes sin and all who do evil.

(42) They will throw them into the blazing furnace, where there will be weeping and gnashing of teeth.

(43) Then the righteous will shine like the sun in the kingdom of their Father. Whoever has ears, let them hear."

A harvester is a machine or organisation that collects resources for future use. The angels will weed out everything that does not represent God, whilst escorting the saints to the place where God prepared them to be. God will send His angels to blow the trumpet that the dead in Christ will hear it.

The angels will gather the elect of God from the north, south-east, and west. The angels will accompany Jesus in the sky while He judges the world, and whatever the outcome of the judgement, the angel will execute it.

If the individual is instructed to go to hell, the angel will take that individual there. If the individual is destined to go to Heaven, the angel will take the individual there. The angels play a major role in the life of men and women from birth to death. Angels will always be at your side fulfilling different assignments throughout your lifetime. Let us not take the ministry of angels for granted. They are here to fulfill the plan of God for humanity.

CHAPTER 8

SALVATION

Call to me, and I will answer you. I will tell you great and mysterious things that you do not know.
Jeremiah 33:3(GWT)

From the moment a person gives their life to Christ, something supernatural takes place whether he or she realises it.

You might have felt goosebumps of the power of God flowing through your body. You may have even fallen out under the power of God, or simply cried tears of joy or awaiting it. When I gave my life to Christ, I encountered a supernatural transaction; an exchange and translation took place. I have been bought with the precious blood of Jesus Christ through His death on the cross which we call redemption.

As we read in Ephesians 1:7 "In Him we have redemption through His blood, the forgiveness of our trespasses, according to the riches of His grace."

I had an exchange because the devil did not want to let go of me. I now belong to Jesus, signifying that the devil has no authority to control my life. My name is written in the Lamb's book of life.

We read in Colossians 1: 12-14 which says: "(12) giving thanks to the Father, who has qualified you to share in the inheritance of the saints in the light. (13) He has rescued us from the dominion of darkness and brought us into the kingdom of His Beloved Son. (14) in whom we have redemption, the forgiveness of sins." Salvation is one of the greatest miracles an individual can ever experience; Salvation is a spiritual rebirth; in other words, spiritual enlightenment causing a person to lead a new life.

Still on the subject of salvation; this is the state of being saved from harm such as the penalty of sin. It is the first supernatural encounter every true believer experiences. If you are truly born again, you have experienced a divine encounter. Other forms of divine encounters include dreams, visions, trances, angelic visitation or the manifestation of the personality of Jesus Christ, God, and the Holy Spirit. Many bible characters had such experiences; many men and women still have had encounters today.

~ CHAPTER 9 ~

THE POWER OF OPENED EYES

Then their eyes were opened, and they recognized him, and he disappeared from their sight –
Luke 24:31(NIV)

To see into the spirit, the Lord has to empower your spiritual eyes to see what He intends for you to see. While the human eye is part of our physical senses, the spiritual eye is part of spiritual senses. The human eye responds to light and pressure. Failure to maintain correct movement can cause severe visual degradation.

God regulates our spiritual eyes, having our mind and hearts tuned to the frequency of heaven which causes our spiritual antenna to pick up things God wants us to see. Moving onto my next point, the reading of God's word is imperative; as the spiritual eyes react to the light of God's word. The more you flood your spirit with the light of God's word, Guess what? You begin to see what you have been exposed to daily.

Why is seeing into the spiritual realm so vital to me? It lets me know when I am in danger and how to avoid it.

Secondly, it lets me know when God is doing something amazing and wants me to have a sneak peek before it manifests in the physical realm. For at least two weeks as a new believer, I was praying this particular prayer:

"O God please let me see an angel even if it's just once."

Days went by, and I saw nothing, so I began reasoning in my mind, maybe this is not going to happen. One night, I woke up at 2.00am. I stood in the middle of the room and began to pray. Suddenly a circle appeared and I saw a man dressed in dazzling white apparel, in a sitting posture with a book and a pen in his hand with one hand on his chin. Even though he was sitting, I could not see a chair. It was as if he was seated in the air and noticed that he was an angel and he had a stern look on his face.

At this point my heart was pounding. I was shaking and was in total shock! I stopped looking at him and began to concentrate on my prayer. He waited for me to say something and will write it down in his book. It was almost as if he was writing my prayer.

The exciting thing about this encounter is that I was always praying to see an angel. When I saw an angel for the first time, I was quite nervous. In the natural realm, I always felt lonely, so to know there was another person in the room and not just anybody but an angel of God, it was very comforting yet nerve-wrecking.

The only way I can describe it is when people encountered angels in the bible where angels would say: "do not be afraid" even though they were bringing good news. Why? Because people did not expect to see them. They are very holy so people were always in shock when they had encounters with such glorious beings.

It was reassuring to know that my prayers were taken to the presence of God. I felt protected by God's holy angel, and nothing could harm me when I finished praying. Then all of a sudden, the angel disappeared, and I was thrilled that God allowed me to see him.

The Power of Open Eyes
Opened eyes and ears greatly enhance your life. When you know the secrets of God:
- You refuse to give up
- You refuse to quit
- You refuse to allow your current circumstances to discourage you.

God will always reveal something to you that will uplift your faith. I am reminded of a vision I had where I saw God sitting on a massive throne next to His right hand; there was also another throne. It was not as big as the Father's throne; Christ was seated on the throne on the right-hand side of the Father.

Jesus Christ said these words to me; "The enemy has desired to sift you like wheat, but I prayed for you that your faith would not fail you". Just like he said to Simon in Luke 22:31.

A few days after having the vision, I lost my job. I was distraught; I asked God why and how I was going to support my children. He reminded me of the vision He showed me previously.

Then it dawned on me that my faith was being tested and had prayed that my faith would not fail me. Eventually, when the time was right, God opened a door for another job which had a higher pay.

But imagine if I had not heard from God to hold onto my faith, the enemy would have had a field day and would discredit me. I could have allowed him to speak into my ear saying: "Listen, God does not care about you…" There are secrets from God which you need to know about as they will turn your life around going forwards.

The benefits of opened eyes:
- Helps you to know who you are
- Helps you to know why you are on this earth
- Helps you to know who your enemy is and their secrets.
- Helps you to discover who your helpers are in life.

~ C H A P T E R 10 ~

I FEEL SAFE

For he will command his angels concerning you to guard you in all your ways -

Psalm 91:11(NIV)

The second angelic visitation was in 2008.It was in the middle of the night while I was sleeping. I saw an angel standing next to the wall. I assumed it was a dream then woke up with excitement! He was such a glorious being. I sat up on my bed and began rubbing my eyes thinking he would not be there. By the time I finished, he was still there.

The angel was dressed in white apparel and was thick and tall. He was standing there smiling at me and did not say a word; I also did not ask him anything either. I prayed to God and went back to bed. I felt safe knowing he was there watching over me, but when I woke in the morning, I did not see him anymore.

~ CHAPTER 11 ~

ANYMORE AND I WILL EXPLODE

By day the Lord went ahead of them in a pillar of cloud to guide them on their way and by night in a pillar of fire to give them light so that they could travel by day or night.
Exodus 13:21 (NIV)

The third angelic visitation was in summer 2009; I had just come home from an opening of a new well- known church. It was an awesome service and I got home quite late and went straight to bed. While I was sleeping around 12:00am, the Lord opened my spiritual eyes to what was taking place in my room and on the ceiling.

There were two angels in the air. It looked like they were giggling. They would look at me and one of them touched the other on the shoulder; they started laughing again. It was beautiful to see the interaction between the two angels when they realized I could see them.

These angels had no wings, and they were human looking; they had white apparel, and their appearances were full of light. I could see through them; they were transparent. One of them pointed his finger towards me and began to release an anointing. While the angel was doing that, I felt my body getting warm and started getting hotter.

I felt as if I was going to explode. I said "Father, anymore of this anointing and I will explode." Immediately I said this, the fire ceased. The Lord reminded me when I was watching a healing service program on YouTube; a man of God speaking to his congregation said whenever the power of God comes on him to heal the sick, he feels he is going to explode.

I remember saying in my heart, if only the power of God will come on me like that and little did I know God already did it with me through His angel. Meanwhile, the angels were still in my room that day. I remember gazing at these angels thinking to myself they are so holy and became afraid. I begged God to stop me from seeing the angels. Immediately I said that, I did not see the angels anymore.

Beloved, God will only reveal His Glory to us on the level which we can obtain. *God will not force himself on us; we must pursue him.*

The cloud on the ceiling

The following week I had similar encounters, but this time I saw a thick white cloud instead of an angel at the ceiling. This cloud released an anointing which looked like lightning; this time I felt God himself visited me.

I was not afraid; in fact I wanted the cloud to stay all day but when I woke up in the morning, the cloud was not there anymore. We read in Exodus 40:34 "Then the cloud covered the tent of meeting, and the Glory of the Lord filled the tabernacle."

~ CHAPTER 12 ~

AND THE HEAVENS WERE OPENED

He then added, very truly I tell you, you will see heaven open, and the angels of God ascending and descending on the Son of Man.

John 1:51 (NIV)

The fourth angelic visitation was in 2014. I have just come back from my 31st December watch night service in 2013, and the power of God was strong during the service. I came back empowered spiritually but tired physically, so I went to bed without praying.

As I slept, I saw a troubling vision that the Lord did not permit me to talk about. The vision troubled me to the extent that I woke up with such urgency to intercede for the person.

I arose and immediately began to pray. The moment I began to pray, the Holy Spirit overshadowed me. I only stopped praying for the person when the Holy Spirit said it was enough.

Immediately when I went back to bed, suddenly I saw the heavens opened, and an angel appeared in the sky with a sword in his hand. This angel had wings, and said to myself what was going on. While I was trying to figure out what was happening, the angel looked at me, and stretched forth his sword. For some reason, I was not afraid. I knew within me that he had been sent to empower me.

This time the anointing was being released through the sword. I felt I was going to explode and was shaking uncontrollably in my bed. The power emanating from the sword looked like lightning entering into my body.

I tell you; it was an eventful night; terrifying yet holy. I watched the angel intensify the anointing by lifting the sword over his right shoulder and stretched it back to me again; I was still shaking. The angel finished and left, and I went back to sleep. That year I faced a lot of challenges, but I give thanks that God was faithful to me. I thank him for being there with me every step of the way and empowering me beforehand to deal with the challenges.

Mary's life completely changed direction after her encounter with the Angel Gabriel:

The Angel Gabriel Comes to Mary

Six months after Elizabeth became pregnant, God sent the Angel Gabriel to Nazareth; a city in Galilee. The angel went to a virgin promised in marriage to a descendant of David named Joseph. The virgin's name was Mary.

When the angel entered her home, he greeted her and said, "The Lord favor is on you! The Lord is with you." She was startled by what the angel said and tried to figure out what this greeting meant. The angel told her, "Don't be afraid, Mary. You have found favor with God. You will become pregnant and will give birth to a son and name him Jesus.

He will be a great man and will be called the Son of the highest. The Lord God will give him the throne of his ancestor David. Your son will be king of Jacob's people forever, and his kingdom will never end." Mary asked the angel, "How can this be? I'm a virgin."

The angel answered her, "The Holy Spirit will come to you, and the power of the Highest will overshadow you. Therefore, the holy child developing inside you will be called the Son of God. "Elizabeth, your relative, is six months pregnant with a son in her old age.

People said she could not have a child. But nothing is impossible for God." Mary answered, "I am the Lord's servant. Let everything you have said happen to me." Then the angel left her.

Imagine how Mary felt like when she had to explain to people that she was pregnant without the help of a man, but God was responsible for her pregnancy. That alone was a challenge, but God came through for her in the end. Divine encounters prepare you for the challenges ahead.

~ CHAPTER 13 ~

THE HOLY SPIRIT

And I will pray for the Father, and he shall give you another
Comforter, that he may abide with you forever.
John 14:16(KJV)

I once heard a pastor say something that drew my attention.
He said when he was discouraged, he would pray while Jesus would sit and encourage him for hours.

I prayed that I would have such an encounter. Going to bed that night I was not expecting to see anything amazing, but suddenly some evil force was trying to overpower me, but immediately the Holy Spirit started declaring Psalm 91 over my life. I saw the Holy Spirit as a bright light and He rose up from my belly, filled my outer body and filled the entire room. The room was so bright that it resisted the evil force.

Within the light, I saw an arm with a dazzling white robe; the hand was outstretched indicating to the evil spirit not to touch me. Eventually, the light became stronger than the enemy, so it left.

"So, shall they fear the name of The Lord from the west and his glory from the rising of the Sun. When the enemy shall come in like a flood, the spirit of the Lord shall lift a standard against him." – Isaiah 59:19(NKJV)

"I know now what the Lord meant when he said my words are Spirit and Life"- (John 6:63)

It is the Spirit who gives life; the words that I have spoken to you are Spirit and Life. This is why it is necessary for us to memorise scriptures because it is not every situation you would have the opportunity use your bible, phone or your tablet for scriptures.

Some situations might demand that you rely on scriptures in your mind and spirit. The Holy Spirit has been sent to remind us that *if our minds are empty of scriptures, we are doing ourselves a disfavour.* As much as the Holy Spirit is here to help us, He will not memorise the scriptures for us; He has His part to play, and so do we.

I also noticed the Holy Spirit likes to sing; there are times where I have heard the Holy Spirit singing over me when I am going through difficult moments in my life. He sings over me as a mother sings over her newborn child.

The songs he sang over me, I have never heard before. I felt empowered to move on with my life. We read in Zephaniah 3:17 that "The LORD, your God, is with you, the Mighty Warrior who saves. He will take great delight in you; in his love, he will no longer rebuke you, but will rejoice over you with singing."

Sometimes, God showed me the outcome of my circumstances that I will have the victory concerning any issue that I face. God truly is my comforter indeed. I love Him so much, and He loves me too!

Whenever I am evangelising, and someone asks a trick question, the Holy Spirit often drops the answer into my spirit. I am amazed at how I came up with such an answer then realised it was the Holy Spirit; I give him all the glory.

When I am asked to minister at church, I like to depend on the Holy Spirit; instead of ministering in my strength which is mostly draining, the Holy Spirit empowers me to sing. He does all the work and all I have to do is yield to Him.

The Holy Spirit
Who is the Holy Spirit?
He is the third person of the Holy Trinity.

Acts 1:8 says: "(8) But you will receive power when the Holy Spirit comes on you, and you will be my witnesses in Jerusalem, and in all Judea and Samaria, and to the ends of the earth."

The Holy Spirit is the power of the anointing. Without the Holy Spirit you can't be anointed. Anointing means to smear or rub with oil. The Holy Spirit is the one who knows the level of anointing we need to minister with.

Whenever I am called to minister, I see the Holy Spirit put His anointing on me. It looked like I'm wrapped in a bubble of Glory and His power protecting me whilst ministering.

No demonic forces will attack me while I am singing or preaching. The anointing makes me bold and helps to forget about my problems, focusing on the task at hand.

The anointing destroys the yoke:
Isaiah 10:27 (KJV) "And it shall come to pass in that day, that his burden shall be taken away from off thy shoulder, and his yoke from off thy neck, and the yoke shall be destroyed because of the anointing."

Some yokes are destroyed when the word of God is being preached: "The word of God is alive and active. Sharper than any double-edged sword, it penetrates even to dividing soul and spirit, joints and marrow; it judges the thoughts and attitudes of the heart. Some yokes are destroyed during prayer, and it's all the work of the Holy Spirit." Hebrews 4:12(NIV)

I remember a time where I saw a man of God of preaching to over 10,000 people. I heard he had been fasting and praying preparing for the service. When he came on stage, I knew God was going to move mightily through him but had no idea what God had in store for his people that night. It was beyond my expectation, and God activated my spiritual senses that I was seeing and feeling somewhat different.

When the man of God came on stage and preached, I saw a glowing sword coming out of his mouth. As he was teaching, I started feeling cold as if I was put in a freezer. I was shaking and saw dazzling white mists everywhere in the auditorium.

I could almost touch it and said to myself if I should ask other people whether they felt the same way, but to my surprise, they didn't. It dawned that God is allowing me to see what is happening in the realm of the spirit while the service was going on. I became quiet and began to observe what God was doing. However, I had an internal dialogue with the Holy Spirit to explain what was going on.

I asked the Holy Spirit why I was feeling cold, and He replied that the healing anointing was being released. As soon the Holy Spirit finished speaking to me, the pastor said those of you who are sick in your body to come forward. I was shocked!

As people who were sick in their body came forward to receive prayer, a young lady in her twenties came forward in the hope of receiving her healing. She had menopause. To have menopause at a young age meant she could not have children when she got married.

This was a severe case where God had to intervene to receive her breakthrough! Before the man of God laid his hands on the woman, the power of God touched the woman's head. It looked like a golden circle ball and immediately, she fell under the power of God. Sometimes, our physical bodies can't contain the power of God!

Then I said to myself "wow!" I know without a shadow of a doubt that God has healed the woman and she can have children. People were being set free from all types of bondages that were incredible to witness.

When going home after the service, I went to bed pondering what took place and how anointed the servant of God was. I had a dream and found myself back at the meeting. This time the man of God was on stage wearing what looked like a graduation gown.

The power of God was on the stage. When I woke up from my sleep, I asked the Lord why the pastor was wearing a graduation gown instead of a tie and suit. The Lord said to me that he was wearing his mantle and that is how it looked in the realm of the spirit.

I did some research on what mantles looked like. I saw a DVD cover with the title 'mantles' and the man on the cover had what seemed like a graduation gown. I said: *"That is what the Lord was trying to show me; I knew what I saw was not just my imagination."*

A mantle serves as a symbolic purpose. It is the priest wrapped in God's authority. In the Old Testament, the coat represents a visible representation of a New Testament principle. The mantle can be seen as a symbol of the anointing of the Holy Spirit.

Prophets were known in the Old Testament for wearing cloaks as a sign of their calling from God. To further reinforce my point, 1 Kings 19:13 says, "When Elijah heard it, he pulled his cloak over his face and went out and stood at the mouth of the cave. Then a voice said to him, "What are you doing here, Elijah?"

Prophet Samuel wore a mantle in reference to 1 Samuel 15:27 (NIV) which reads: "(27) As Samuel turned to leave, Saul caught hold of the hem of his robe, and it tore. The prophet Elijah "threw his cloak around Elisha" as a symbol of Elijah's ministry being passed onto Elisha.

The prophet's mantle was an indication of his authority and responsibility as God's chosen spokesman in reference to 2 Kings 2:8. Elisha was not confused as to what Elijah was doing; the putting on of his mantle made his election clear.

On that note, I would like to ask: "Have you received the Holy Spirit?" I pray you receive the Holy Spirit in Jesus Name. AMEN!

THE KING OF KINGS - JESUS CHRIST OF NAZARETH

And on His robe and His thigh, He has a name written,
"KING OF KINGS, AND LORD OF LORDS".
Revelation 19:16(NIV)

The Lord showed me a vision standing in a park and was singing a new song to God. I didn't see the heavens open, but I did see my song penetrating through the sky. It was in the form of a bright light going to God. The park was full of white chairs with young ladies sitting on them. When I finished singing, they all stood up and clapped so fast, it looked like someone fast-forwarded them.

When I woke up the next morning, I asked God what the dream meant. He wanted me to hold a conference for young ladies in my community. I decided to go ahead with what God had asked me to do. While I was planning the event, I didn't know how I was going to pay for it. The following week, I was crying after I came back from Wednesday prayer meeting.

I went to bed really down that night. In my sleep, I saw an incredible vision; Jesus Christ was dressed in a white robe, with a red sash and a golden crown sitting on a throne. I was so excited as I've always wanted to see Jesus.

During the vision, I saw Jesus Christ as a King. Jesus was talking to me and making hand gestures. His lips were moving, but I could not hear what He was saying. As I looked down, I saw a lot of people dancing and shouting in my living room. I told them to be quiet! Jesus Christ is speaking, and I can't hear him.

Jesus pointed at my computer. I looked at the screen and whatever He was saying was appearing in a typed format. I started reading it. The words said: "I will help you". The dream ended and I woke up. I was distraught because I didn't see Him after that and wanted Him to tell me more. The following morning, I asked God what the dream meant, and He said, "I will help you with the convention."

Since that encounter, my spirit was encouraged. God started sending people to help me financially. Resources came from every direction; people offering to help and eventually held the event at the park.

I hired white chairs; a marquee, speakers, the stage, and gospel artists who came to minister. The whole conference was successful. God was glorified, and the young ladies were blessed.

Beloved, I just want to take this opportunity to encourage you that whenever God gives you a vision, He will always help you to fulfil it; just put your trust in His hands.

~ C H A P T E R 15 ~

THE KING OF GLORY

His eyes are like blazing fire, and on his head, are many crowns. He has a name written on him that no one knows but him himself.

Revelation 19:12(NIV)

The second time I saw Jesus the King of Glory, in this particular vision, I found myself standing in front of Jesus gazing at His excellent Glory. I was immediately taken to my Wednesday prayer meeting which was held at a woman's house.

I noticed everyone at the meeting was sitting on a sofa chatting. It looked like they had finished praying. I walked past everyone in the room and went towards the window, lifted up the curtains and looked outside. It was dark because it was towards evening. I put my head through the window and screamed JESUS!

I found myself right back in the presence of Jesus. He was sitting on a throne wearing a white robe, a gold sash with a golden crown, and the glory of God was pulsating through His entire being. Everywhere was full of beauty.

His eyes blazing with coals of fire were awe-striking to see. I was not afraid. When He spoke to me, His voice was tender and gentle. He said, "Vivianne! The church (referring to the people at the prayer meeting) has prayed, but they have not asked for anything. Go back and ask them what they want so I can do it for them."

I found myself right back in the woman's house where the prayer meeting was taking place. I began telling the group that Jesus informed them that they prayed but haven't asked Him for anything. Tell me what you want, and I will go back to inform Jesus. The leader of the cell group said, "Jesus, we want mercy and grace". After she stated that, I found myself back in the presence of Jesus. I told him what the lady had said, her prayer was answered.

This vision taught me that we have to pray according to the will of the Father, because most times when we Christian pray, we can pray amiss. This is described in James 4:3 AMP which reads: (3) You ask God for something and do not receive it because you ask with wrong motives [out of selfishness or with an unrighteous agenda] so that [when you get what you want you may spend it on your hedonistic desires."

This verse sums it up, which further reinforces my point.

My third encounter was in a vision where Jesus was standing in front of the church. He demonstrated the link between the word of knowledge that goes forth and when the person is being healed. I saw Master Jesus dressed in a white robe with a red sash across his robe. He was touching the shoulder of a lady who had come forward to be prayed over concerning a particular condition.

Jesus would use His eyes to scan through the body like an x-ray machine to identify where the sickness was. As soon as His eyes recognized the condition, immediately the person was healed instantly. I noticed the pastor saying in the vision by word of knowledge that a woman is now being healed of from her condition.

This vision revealed Jesus Christ as the healer and not the man (in this case the Pastor). *This is why we should not take credit for what God does through us.* These next chapters are flashes, not great visions like what I have described in the chapters above.

As you are well aware during the reading of this book, the Holy Spirit woke me up to pray at 2.00am. However, at this particular time, I was having trouble waking up due to tiredness. I decided to sleep for five more minutes.

Immediately, I saw a staircase which touched Heaven and its base was on the earth. I saw Jesus walking back to Heaven dressed in His Majestic white robe. It was thick and long, and I noticed He was holding the end of his robe so he could climb the stairs properly.

It seemed that He had a sad look on His face. I immediately realised He'd been sitting beside my bed waiting for me to wake up and pray. He wanted me to spend quality time with Him, but instead, I was busy enjoying my sleep. I rose up quickly from my bed and said "Please Jesus, come back! Come back, please! I will pray! I am up now."

Beloved, just because we do not see Him, does not mean He is not there. He enjoys fellowshipping with us. Let us always make time to fellowship with Him. When we spend time with Him, we come out with destiny, purpose, and a strategy on how to be victorious in life.

Another scenario: I was sleeping and had to pray but was feeling tired. I saw Jesus in a vision standing next to a tree. It looked like the tree was in a forest. He was holding the trunk of a particular tree and was listening to my internal dialog whilst I was sleeping. I was saying "Jesus, I need to pray, but my body is tired; can you pray for me instead please?"

He just shook his head with a smile as to say: "No, you have to do it yourself." I realise praying for myself helped me develop my "spiritual muscles" which no one could do for me. I had to discipline myself to the point where prayer became a lifestyle, which built a meaningful relationship with God.

From then on, my prayer life went to another level. I took my prayers more seriously and realized what goes on during prayer, that God is using my prayers to download the vision and dreams into my spirit.

My prayer life equips me to win spiritual warfare. Whenever I prayed and found myself being attacked, my boldness in rebuking the enemy was much stronger; I rebuked him with strong force and authority. On the flip side, I noticed that when I did not pray, I felt weak; this is where the enemy has a field day.

This does not happen when I pray, however. Why? Because God knows what the enemy has planned, therefore, He equips and empowers us to fight (every) spiritual warfare we are going to face. Isaiah 40:31 says: "But they that wait upon the Lord shall renew their strength; they shall mount up with wings as eagles; they shall run, and not be weary, and they shall walk, and not faint."

~ CHAPTER 16 ~

THE SERVANT KING

"For even the Son of Man did not come to be served, but to serve, and to give His life a ransom for many" -
Mark 10:45(NIV)

I had a dream and saw a group of people sitting in a restaurant setting dressed in white gowns. Jesus was also dressed in a white robe holding a tray with expensive silver cups. He was balancing the tray with His hand and was giving everyone a drink from it, eventually the dream ended.

This next vision of Jesus was compelling due to what it symbolised. In this particular vision, I saw Jesus standing a few feet from the Cross; there was no one on the Cross. Jesus was dressed in a cream robe and while He was standing there, He looked up to the Cross and turned His head sideways looking downwards. The look on Christ's face was almost as if He was reflecting on how He suffered on that day of His crucifixion. *I just want us to think about that for a minute...*

The following song brings our attention to the servanthood of Christ
"He is the servant King; this song describes Him as a

servant King:
The Servant King (From Heaven you came)
From Heaven, you came a helpless babe
Entered our world, your glory veiled
not to be served but to serve
and gave your life that we might live
This is our God; The Servant King
He calls us now to follow Him
to bring our lives as a daily offering
of worship to The Servant King
There in the garden of tears
my heavy load he chose to bear
His heart with sorrow was torn
'yet not my will but yours,' He said
See His hands and His feet
the scars that speak of sacrifice
Hands that flung stars into space
to cruel nails surrendered
So, let us learn how to serve
and in our lives, enthrone Him
Each other's needs to prefer
for it is Christ, we're serving."
Written by Graham Kendrick

One of the reasons for writing this book is to show young people that God is real and needs to experience the raw power of God. I hope this book empowers this generation to see God on another level and would not be ashamed to seek God with all their heart.

With this in mind, I remember having a vision where a group of young people harassed the entire community with knives to the point where people were avoiding these gang members. The gangs would come to church; members tried hiding from them. I remember standing in a little box and saw the gang members looking tired, lying next to a tree.

I began ministering to them about how real God is, and said He could change their life for the better. I asked God to show me how I could let these boys know how true He is, and what I received was the story about Prophet Elijah who called down fire from heaven to prove to the people of Israel that the Lord of Israel is God.

I saw myself standing in the box and I remember looking up to Heaven and I said to God, "Please let these boys see how real you are."

Immediately I said that God told me to speak in tongues, and within minutes, I became transparent. In this vision the power came from Heaven and hit my stomach; it looked like flashes of lightning.

The boys could see what God was doing to me in the vision and were in shock! With their mouth wide opened, they said: "It's okay, it's okay we get it! God is real; we are going to serve God from now on." The moment the boys said that, God dropped me back in the box and the boys threw their knives in a skip until it couldn't contain any more knives. That is what the raw power of God can do!

Nowadays, the Gospel has been watered down, and as a result, we do not experience the power of God like in days of the Act of the Apostles.

DL Moody showed this raw power by just being on a train. When the raw power hit the train and everyone on-board began to cry concerning their sins repenting before God, people asked: "What is going on?". A lady replied, "it looks like DL Moody is in town."

The only way to bring down crime is not by using different government policies, rather the church going back to the place of power. Only the power of God can make this generation love God!

~ CHAPTER 17 ~

AN APPOINTMENT WITH ALMIGHTY GOD

Have I not commanded you? Be strong and courageous. Do not be afraid; do not be discouraged, for the Lord your God will be with you wherever you go.
Joshua 1:9 (NIV)

In 2009, I went to bed every other night, but this was set to be a night I would never forget. While I was sleeping, whether I was in the body or out of my body, I do not know. Suddenly, I was taken into the presence of Almighty God.

I found myself lying face down on a solid surface and on my left side, I saw a little tree and leaves that were green on the branches, quite similar to the ones seen in the films when Moses approaches the burning bush. Just a little further on my right side, I saw a very bright light.

I could tell it was a mighty light; very powerful. I had a sense that God was expecting me, even though I was surprised to be there, He was not.

I felt His overwhelming love and had an awareness of how Holy he is, He was covered in a cloud of glory and could see where the light of Glory began. I could not see the end because the light goes further into eternity. For example, when you go to the seaside, you know where the sea begins, but you cannot see where the sea ends; instead, it looked like the sky was touching the sea from a far distance.

If you went on a ship and decided to investigate as you travel on the sea, you will get closer and discover that the sky is not connected to the sea at all. You will realise the sea goes into other countries and the sky was not attached to the sea.

In the same way, the light of God covers the entire heavens and beyond, which I call it infinity or eternity; almost as if His Glory goes into another world. My friends, God is indeed powerful; more than you can ever imagine. No human adjective in the English dictionary can accurately describe how Holy, Awesome and Beautiful our God is; He is an indescribable God!

That is why when angels cry out "Holy to Lord Almighty!" They do not say it once, they say it thrice, Holy, Holy, Holy is the Lord God Almighty, emphasizing on how Holy God is.

The Bible says that He sits enthroned above the circle of the earth, and His train fills the temple. I used to wonder how His train fills the entire Heavens; His glory fills the whole of Heaven. 1 John 1-5 tells us a message heard from Jesus; I now declare to you; God is light, and there is no darkness in Him at all.

Back to my vision: while lying in the presence of Almighty God, my hands covered my face, and a holy fear came on me. Before this encounter, I had not seen God prior to that,so my initial responses were questioning where I was at the time. I said these exact words to myself "What is that?"

Immediately, my spirit knew where I was, but my mind was having trouble keeping up. I could sense deep down within me that I was in the presence of someone Glorious, Holy and Powerful.

God wraps himself in light and Glory, so I could not see His features, but I felt energy emanating from Him which was like fire.

Holiness is the very essence of who God is, He is very Holy. The energy emanating from God felt like fire.

This is the fire we ask for when we pray to God: "I want your fire". His fire brings life, empowers us to do well and energises us.

I noticed I was covering my eyes at a point because He was too Holy and too Bright to look upon. I was peeping through my fingers to see His Glory. I took my hands off for a few seconds to behold his Glory in all its fullness and immediately covered my eyes again.

Beloved, God is so glorious and awesome to look upon. He did not say anything but felt like He was gazing down at me with a proud look. I could sense I was having a father and daughter moment with my Heavenly Father, even though He was wrapped in his Glory without seeing His features. I could feel His presence and His overwhelming love.

God loves us so much, and if you are reading this book and feel far away, please know that He loves you more than you can imagine, more than your human father or mother could.

God is not distant or angry with you; He wants to give your life meaning and purpose.
If you knew my testimony, you would think why God would want anything to do with me, but He wanted me and allowed me to see Him face to face. God is our loving Abba Father. You are not a mistake, and God has a plan for your life.

God is the Alpha and Omega; He is the beginning and the end, meaning He knows the end from the beginning.

God has gone to the end of your life, and your end will be glorious because He brought you to this earth to live it out.

After my encounter, I woke up the next day wondering and thinking about what or who I just saw. Within seconds a verse dropped in my spirit. "Those who are pure in heart will see God" Matthew 5:8. It is an honour to see God, the invincible God.

This brought so much joy to my heart that I jumped out of my bed in such a rush, ran down to the living room calling my dad, I yelled: "Dad! Dad! 'you won't believe who I saw in my dream today!" My dad understands that I dream a lot.

He was wondering what it was this time and said to him I saw God. His first response was: "What! 'What do you mean you saw God'"? I began to describe the vision to him. The verse the Holy Spirit put in my spirit came up. He was in shock, to say the least, and was amazed that God revealed Himself to me that way. By this time, I was running around the house with such joy and excitement, praising and thanking God for allowing me to see Him.

Before this great encounter, my favorite verse was when Moses saw God face to face. I used to ponder on how God revealed Himself to Moses, and He still lived after the encounter.

In reference to this, it says in Exodus 33:11-23 (KJV):

"(11) And the Lord spake unto Moses face to face, as a man speaketh unto his friend. And he turned again into the camp: but his servant Joshua, the son of Nun, a young man, departed not out of the tabernacle.

(12)   And Moses said unto the Lord, See, thou sayest unto me, bring up this person: and thou hast not let me know whom thou wilt send with me. Thou hast said, I know thee by name, and thou hast also found grace in my sight.

(13)   Now, therefore, I pray thee, if I have found grace in thy sight, show me now thy way, which I may know thee, that I may find grace in thy sight and consider that this nation is thy people.

(14)   And he said my presence should go with thee, and I will give the rest.

(15)   And he said unto him, if thy presence goes not with me, carry us not up hence.

(16)   For wherein shall it be known here that the people and I have found grace in thy sight? Is it not in that thou goes with us? So, shall we be separated, I and thy people, from all the people that are upon the face of the earth?

(17)   And the Lord said unto Moses; I will do this thing also that thou hast spoken: for thou hast found grace in my sight, and I know thee by name.

(18)	And he said, I beseech thee, shew me thy glory.

(19)	And he said, I will make all my goodness pass before thee, and I will proclaim the name of the Lord before thee; and will be gracious to whom I will be gracious and will shew mercy on whom I will shew mercy.

(20)	And he said thou canst not see my face: for there shall no man see me, and live.

(21)	And the Lord said, Behold, there is a place by me, and thou shalt stand upon a rock

(22)	And it shall come to pass, while my glory passed by, that I will put thee in a cliff of the rock, and will cover thee with my hand while I pass by

(23)	And I will take away my hand, and thou shalt see my back parts: but my face shall not be seen."

Even though God's Holiness could have consumed Moses, God spared his life because Moses asked to know God's way. This touches God's heart so much that He went beyond what Moses asked for. God revealed His goodness and proclaimed who Moses was, because he asked God for it. *God is longing to reveal Himself to us, but we need to ask Him.*

I read this verse for a long time and is one of my favorite verses in the Bible. I've always wondered, why God revealed Himself to Moses and spared his life. Little did I know He would show Himself to me and save my life too.

As he said in His word, *"I will be gracious to whom I will be gracious, and I will show me mercy to whom I will show mercy." Exodus 33:19.(NLT)* God is no respecter of persons. He loves us all the same!

During the vision, God could see right through me, and He didn't say a word. I didn't ask Him any questions either; rather, He allowed me to feel his overwhelming love which was pure.
The reason why I am telling you this is to let you know that God loves you. You don't have to be perfect before He is pleased with you. He just wants a relationship with you. God was pleased with Jesus, even before His wilderness experience, healing the sick, and dying on the cross to save humanity. My advice to you, beloved, is to desire a revelation about who God is, rather than another person's revelation of who God is.

You might ask yourself: "how do I get revelations of who God is?" God reveals Himself to you in the language you understand. In other words, if you haven't experienced a father figure in your life, He would prove himself to you; to be a father to the fatherless. If you struggle financially, He will show Himself as the great provider.

If you are fearful, He will let you know He is your shield and strong tower. Jeremiah 33:3 says "Seek me with all your heart, and you find me, and I will show you tremendous and mighty things you do not know off". Spend time reading your Bible and pray more often!

CHAPTER 18

THE ULTIMATE ROYAL FAMILY

*But you are a chosen people, a royal priesthood, a holy nation,
God's special possession, that you may declare the praises of
Him who called you out of darkness into His marvelous light -
1 Peter 2:9(NIV)*

Why did God allow me to experience such divine
encounters? I believe as Christians; the bible says we
have been adopted into the royal family of God. Do we
fully understand what it means to be part of the
Kingdom of God?

These are questions we need to ask ourselves to help us
grasp the concept of the Kingdom of Heaven and
embrace our new identity as a royal priesthood. First, we
need to find out what a Kingdom is and how it operates.

I live in the United Kingdom with a monarchy, so I
understand the concept of a royal family. With that said,
there are democratic governments who are responsible
for making concrete decisions regarding the affairs of the
nation.

I only see the royal family during special occasions including royal weddings, royal tours, the Queen's speech; to name a few. I don't see the royal family exercising its authority like in the days of old.

Other parts of the world are familiar with the democratic governments and become part of the royal family of God. They mistakenly interpret the Kingdom of God as a democratic state.

When Jesus Christ revealed himself to me as a King, He stirred up a desire to know more about Him and His Kingdom. I began to study more about what Kingdom meant by listening to preachers. I understood that I am a citizen and an ambassador of the Kingdom of God; you are too!

We are sent here to influence the earth for Christ through the help of the Holy Spirit, bringing the culture of Heaven down on earth. For example, there is no sickness or diseases in Heaven, so we need to take the healing power of Jesus to the world. We cannot sit on the anointing that God has given us; we need to use it to help humanity and glorify God.

Secondly, a Kingdom is a king's domain - A king has dominion; his power governs a nation. This reminds me of the scripture in Genesis 1:26 which says "Then God said, 'Let us make man in our image, after our likeness. And let them have dominion over the fish of the sea and the birds of the heavens and the livestock and all the earth and over every creeping thing that creeps on the earth."

We are kings and God has given us a dominion mandate which is to rule and reign in life. Every kingdom must have a king or queen. It is also true that every king is "Lord" whilst a president, prime minister, mayor or a governor must be voted into power/positions.

Kings and queens are born to inherit power, and from the moment they are born they are treated like royalty and trained to handle several positions they will inherit at the appropriate time. A king or queen's lordship makes him different from any other kind of leader.

Jesus spent His entire life on earth talking about the Kingdom; He was bringing to light how things operate in heaven.

Third, kings are supposed to care for the welfare of their subjects
- Our King, Jesus Christ, certainly takes care of us to the point where He died for us.

A kingdom consists of the following:

1.   A King
2.   The Territory
3.   The Constitution
4.   The Citizens
5.   The Law
6.   The Privileges
7.   The Code of Conduct
8.   The Army
9.   The Commonwealth
10.   The Culture

A King

A Kingdom is the glory of the king - The king's word or decree is the seal by his signet ring; a seal which cannot be broken. If this applies to an earthly king, how much more the word of the Almighty God.

The Territory

The Territory is the domain over which the king exercises his authority - The territory, its resources, and people are subject to the king's authority. The king by right owns everything subject to him. The word Lord means owner. The Scripture declares in Psalm 24:1 "*The Earth is the Lord's and all its fullness, the world and those who dwell there in it.*"

The Lord Jesus Christ owns us; we are not our own so we ought to live our lives according to God's agenda, not our agenda.

The Constitution

The Constitution is the expressive mind and will of the king for his citizens and the kingdom - The constitution is the documented words of the king. The Bible is the constitution of the Kingdom of God which details His will and mind for His citizens.

The Citizens

The Citizens are the subject of the king, and they live under the king's authority - Once an individual is born into a kingdom, the person is a citizen. The benefits and the privileges of a nation are only accessible to the citizens. A citizen of the Kingdom of God benefits from everything God has to offer.

The Law

The Law constitutes principles established by a king himself, by which his kingdom will be ruled - The laws of a country are to be obeyed by all, including citizens and foreigners living in it. Violations of the law will bring punishment to the offender. Citizens cannot change the legislation in a kingdom.

The Privileges

The Privileges are the benefits a king and his kingdom have to offer its citizens - The privileges of the Kingdom of Heaven: salvation, divine provision, protection, long life, prosperity, the opportunity of becoming a joint heir with Christ and finally spending eternity with Christ.

The Code of Conduct

The Code of Conduct is the appropriate conduct of the citizens in the kingdom and their representation of the kingdom - This code comprises the right standards, community relationships, and individual behavior.

The Army

An Army is the defending system of the kingdom - In the kingdom of God, armies are the angels of God, also known as the armies of the Living God or the Hosts of Heaven. The word *host* means army and identifies angels as the military component of the Kingdom of Heaven.

The Bible says that Archangel Michael commands the army of the Living God and Michael fought against the rebel forces of Satan in Heaven. As a celestial Prince of Israel, he accompanied the children of Israel whenever they went to war, even though at times they did not know that he was with them, except for one occasion where he revealed himself to Joshua.

Joshua was once near Jericho. He looked up and saw a man standing before him with a drawn sword in his hand. Joshua went to him and said, "Are you for us or against us"? He replied, "Neither, but as commander of the army of the Lord I have now come". Joshua fell on his face to the earth and worshipped. He said to him, "what do you command your servant, my Lord?" The commander of the army of the Lord said to Joshua, "Remove the sandals from your feet, for the place where you stand is holy". And Joshua did so.

This verse shows that the angels do not battle in the heavenly realm, but they help in fighting our earthly battles. Ultimately, the battle is the Lord's. The army of Heaven assists us during prayer to fight against any demonic force that would try to attack us.

The Book of Joshua 5:13-15 talks about Joshua encountering a *"captain of the host of the Lord"* on his quest to possess the Promised Land. This heavenly messenger is sent by God to encourage Joshua in the upcoming claiming of the Promised Land:

In 2 King 6:17, Elisha prayed, "Open his eyes, LORD, so that he may see". Then the LORD opened the servant's eyes, and he looked and saw the hills full of horses and chariots of fire all around Elisha.

Psalm 103:20-21 says: "Bless the Lord, you His angels, who excel in strength, who do His word. Bless the Lord, all you His hosts, you minister of His, who do His pleasure"

A Commonwealth

A Commonwealth is the economic system of the kingdom - the term commonwealth is used because the king desires that all his citizens share and benefit from the wealth of the kingdom.

Luke 12-31-32 says: "But seek the Kingdom of God, and all these things shall be added to you. Do not fear, little flock, for it is your Father's good pleasure to give you the kingdom.
In the kingdom of God, it is God's Will that we prosper and be in good health even as our souls prospers."

The Culture

The Culture is created by the lifestyle of the king and its citizens
- Their culture separates and distinguishes them from any other kingdom. A typical example is when the children of Israel were told to only worship the one true God, and that set them apart from the nearby countries who were pagan worshippers.

The culture of Holiness and praising God separates the Kingdom from darkness. The culture of the kingdom of darkness is evident in the words of the Lord Jesus. The enemy came to steal and destroy, but I have come that you may have life and have it more abundantly (John 10:10).

God said in Genesis 1:26-28: "(26) Then God said, "Let us make mankind in our image, in our likeness, so that they may rule over the fish in the sea and the birds in the sky, over the livestock and all the wild animals, and over all the creatures that move along the ground.

(27)   So, God created man in his image, in the image of God created ; male and female created them.

(28)   And God blessed them, and God said unto them, be fruitful, and multiply, and replenish the earth, and subdue it: and have dominion over the fish of the sea, and over the fowl of the air, and over every living thing that moves upon the earth.

This verse implies humanity that has been given a dominion mandate.

What is the mandate

To be fruitful, multiply, replenish and subdue - This dominion mandate is to rule in our sphere of influence, the fish of the sea, the birds of air and earth. The authority is not given to dominate people. *Why?* God told us to love one another. We are all kings; Jesus is the king of kings; we are "small kings". The dominion mandate is not for just a group of people; it is for every human being on the earth, so do not allow people to discourage you, rather tap into the king inside you by growing in the knowledge and understanding of the word of God.

For my people are destroyed for lack of knowledge; our biggest demise is lack of knowledge. Darkness means the absence of light. By studying the word, we acquire the knowledge we need.

The word is Christ

The Greek translation for "word" is logos, which means

Being the expression of thought; a saying - The Scripture is the manifestation of God's thoughts in word and the flesh, Jesus says my words are spirit and life and when you see me, you have seen the Father.

If we are not studying the word of God, how can we possibly demonstrate the kingship that has been bestowed upon us? We as the body of Christ need to rise in our identity to dominate the kingdoms of this world until they become the Kingdom of our God and of His Christ.

~ CHAPTER 19 ~

How TO ACTIVATE YOUR SPIRITUAL SENSES

*But strong meat belongeth to them that are of full age,
even those who by reason of use have their senses exercised
to discern both good and evil.*
Hebrews 5:14(KJV)

Just as the body has five senses to interact with the physical world, so does our Spirit. It has five senses which interact with the spiritual realm.

John 4:6-30 states that the true worshipers shall worship the Father in Spirit and truth for the Father seeks such worshippers.

We access God through our spirit including:
• The human being consists of a spirit, soul, and body.
• The spirit is the God-conscious part of us.
• The soul stimulates the body.
• The body interacts with the physical realm.
• The spirit has sight, smell, touch, sound, speech, and taste.
• The soul is our will, mind, and emotions.

- The body is a house or a temple where the soul and the spirit reside.

The soul of man

The Hebrew word for soul is *Nephesh,* translated means *breathing*:

1. The breathing being or living being.
2. The soul is the mind, will, and emotion.
3. The soul consists of our passions, appetites, consciousness, and desires.
4. It is what makes you unique and different from other people.

The spirit of man

1. The spirit reflects the image or likeness of God.
2. The spirit is God's conscious part of you.
3. The spirit can interact with the supernatural.
4. The Holy Spirit is within our spirit.

The Bible says God has hidden eternity in our heart. Therefore, the Kingdom of God is within us. *We are not human beings having a temporary spiritual experience, but we are spiritual beings having a temporary human experience.*

You can train your spiritual senses as well. This is stated in Hebrew 5:14(NIV) which reads: "Solid food is for those who are mature, who through training have the skill to recognize the difference between right and wrong."

Steps to developing Spiritual Senses
o   Be aware of your spirit and the Holy Spirit.
o   Feed your spirit with the word of God.
o   Exercise your spirit by praying in your understanding and the spirit.
o   Live by the spirit, not the flesh.
o   Guard your heart with all diligence.
o   Live a life of intersection.
o   Consecrate yourself.
o   Live a life of worship.

Close the Gates
o   Eye Gate – What you watch.
o   Ear Gate - What you listen to.
o   Mouth Gate - What you say.

These gates lead directly to your soul, and if whatever is filtering through these gates are negative, they will contaminate the mind and spirit.

"Whatever things are true, whatever things are noble, whatever things are just, whatever things are pure, whatever things are lovely, whatever things are of good report, if there is any virtue and if there is anything praiseworthy, meditate on these things" - Philippians 4:8(KJV).

You were designed to live in the glorious realm, and the more you spend time fellowshipping with God, you will live life in what we call the *glory realm.*

God desires for us to express our God-like nature adequately. *The whole earth is eagerly waiting for the manifestation of the sons of God.*

Matthew 13:13-17 says: "But blessed are your eyes because they see and your ears because they hear. For I tell you the truth, many prophets and righteous men longed to see what you see but did not see it and to listen to what you hear but did not listen to it. It is not a thing of the past. Jesus Christ is the same yesterday, today and forever.

The more time we spend time with God either in prayer, studying the Bible, worshiping and consecration, the closer we get to Him. The more He will reveal himself to us.

Prayer
How Often Should We Pray?
Pray without ceasing! Praying always in the Spirit with all prayer and supplication 1 Thessalonians 5:17(KJV).

Worshipping

About midnight, Paul and Silas were praying and singing hymns to God. The Bible tells of entering it into His gates with thanksgiving and into his court with praise Psalm 100:4(ESV).

What Should We Pray For?

Intercession:

To that end, keep alert with all perseverance, making supplication for all the saints, in Christ Jesus. Pray for lost souls to come to the knowledge of Jesus Christ. Romans 10:1 says: "Brothers, my heart's desire and prayer is that they may be saved."

Personal Prayer

Personal prayer is where you petition before the throne of God for Him to intervene in your affairs. Psalm 118:25 says: "Save us, we pray, O LORD! O LORD, we pray, give us success!"

Pray with the Word of God

Scripture tells us the word of God is living and active, sharper than any double-edged sword, piercing until it divides soul and spirit, joints and marrow, as it judges the thoughts and purposes of the heart - Hebrews 4:12.

Whether it's reminding God of His word or destroying the work of the enemy with the sword of the Spirit. The word of God is one of the most effective weapons we engage in prayer with. Take salvation as your helmet and the word of God as the sword the Spirit supplies in reference to Ephesians 6:18.

Psalm 119:15-16(NLT)says:"I will study your commandments and reflect on your ways. I will delight in your decrees and not forget your word."

Consecration

God told Joshua to tell the people of Israel, "Consecrate yourselves, for tomorrow the Lord will do amazing things for you" - Joshua 3:5

What is consecration?

Consecration is defined as an act of dedicating oneself to a purpose. To consecrate means to commit yourself to something to the greatest significant.

Devoting your life entirely to God

A person can be consecrated to the things of God. For example, being ordained as a Minister, Pastor, Bishop, Prophet, or Apostle, you can have your act of dedication to God. To consecrate a thing or person is to make that thing or individual Holy.

The concept of devotion was first mentioned in the book of Joshua; the Lord told Joshua He was about to visit his people and they needed to consecrate themselves because He was going to perform great and mighty miracles among them. He did not want any of them to miss out on it!

Consecration is a spiritual act and a form of discipline which is subjecting your Heart, Spirit, Soul, and Body to achieve a greater purpose, which is to draw closer to God and be able to do all that God has called us to be:

- Your heart is where the issues of life come from.
- The spirit is the God-conscious part of you.
- The soul is what makes you unique from everyone else.
- The body is what helps you to interact with this world using our five physical senses.

Even though grace saves us through faith, we still need to apply the word of God which says be Holy as I am Holy. This is a conscious effort to live a life of Holiness. The act of consecration is also referred to in the New Testament. Similarly, in Romans 12:1-2 Paul describes the necessity of viewing the body as a living sacrifice to God.

THE SECRET OF GOD

The Secret of the Lord is with those who fear Him; He will let them know His covenant and reveal to them it's meaning -Psalm 25:14. The verse describes how God has a secret, and not everyone will know of it, unless they draw closer to Him.

God also has a covenant, and only those who enter the covenant with Him will know the secret. When you become a child of God, He begins to tell you His secrets. Surely the Lord God will do nothing except to reveal His secrets to His servants in reference to
Amos 3:7.

Surely the Sovereign LORD does nothing without revealing His plan to His servants, the prophets. Believe it or not but there are people around you the Lord has revealed certain secrets to, regarding what will happen in the economy, politics, our countries and so much more!

The Supreme Court of Heaven

I had a vision about the supreme court of Heaven where God is the Judge, Jesus Christ is the advocate and the angel with a big book in his hand.

Before my visitation to the Supreme Court of Heaven, I was told at work not to come back again. I was wondering why. To my knowledge I did nothing wrong and was working within the family support sector. The council gave me a contract and it was to support a particular family. This was fine until the family found out I was a Christian. The family I was assigned to were Muslims.

I did everything I was asked to do, and when the lady rang and informed me not to come back, I was broken because I worried about my children and how I was going to look after them. I forgot about the matter days later and didn't have time to cry. I immediately started looking for another job.

Glory be to God, I got a new job almost immediately.

A month into my new job, I went to bed one particular night, and had a vision. It was as if God was showing me the reason why I lost my previous Job.

I found myself in the house of the Muslim family I was supporting previously. I asked them why they fired me; the husband of the lady said, "because you are a Christian!". I was shocked! I asked them "is that all?," to which he responded: "Yes!".

I found myself in the council building; I said these exact words: "why didn't the council find the reason behind this couple firing me?" I said these words in the vision and summoned the council to the supreme court of Heaven. It was a very Holy sight; everything was as if we were in a courtroom except this wasn't just any court, it was God who was in charge.

Instead of pleading my case, I began to complain. I found myself right back on earth in the council building and stopped complaining. I summoned the council to the supreme court of Heaven, then found myself back in the supreme court of Heaven again. After that, the vision ended.

A few months after the vision, I had a new contract from the council to be a Contact Supervisor for two different boroughs.
God vindicated and gave me a higher position than my previous role.

God is our vindicator, and when we place our case before Him, He deals with our case almost immediately. Just because we cannot see Him at work does not mean He is not working on our behalf. Let us hold on to His word, and He will undoubtedly come through for us.

The effects of social media in our Christian lives

I have a picture of King Jesus on my phone. I have also downloaded many apps as the majority of us do from time to time. These apps cover the picture of Jesus, which I use as my wallpaper. I cannot remember which day it was, but as I was about to pray, and I saw a quick vision of Jesus moving the apps like someone drawing a curtain. He was moving the apps to one side to stop it from blocking His face.

The vision ended. It dawned on me that I have been spending too much time on my phone, instead of spending time with God. I believe Jesus showed me that vision to make a point.

Although social media helps us to reach the masses, we have access to other people's lives and allows us to express our opinion on videos, websites and blogs which gives us a chance to promote our brands. Social media is becoming addictive which in turn, is becoming a distraction to many of us.

We need to start spending more time with God. He is trying to reach out to us, but we are busy with social media that we can't see or hear him trying to reach out to us. The radio station is always on, but until you tune into the frequency of the radio, that is when you begin to hear the program on the station clearly.

There are times in our lives where we find ourselves posting highlights and not posting our moments of weakness; in other words, being transparent. We leave the impression that everything is going great in our lives, when really, we are broken and discouraged. We assume that others are also having a better life than us. We are all the same and we hurt differently.

Social media can become addictive, particularly for people's approval. This at times makes us forget the only approval which ultimately matters, which is God alone! Social media can be a time waster that should be used to serve God and fellowship with Him.

Social media can also create a sense of competition; people doing whatever they can to get more likes, attention and notifications. It leaves a sense of inadequacy, seeing people portraying what appears to be a successful lifestyle can leave a person feeling like a failure and inadequate to achieve that kind of lifestyle.

Social media introduced a new trend called "'Selfie".
This *selfie* is fulfilling the prophecy in 2 Timothy 3:1-3 which reads:

(1)   But understand this: In the last days, difficult times will come.

(2).   For men will be lovers of themselves, lovers of money, boastful, arrogant, abusive, and disobedient to their parents, ungrateful, unholy.
(3).   Unloving, unforgiving, slanderous, without self-control, brutal, without the love of good.

Lovers of themselves means to only focus and see yourself better than others. As Christians, we need to be wise and strategic on how we use social media. Do we use social media to glorify ourselves or do we use it to glorify Jesus?

Social media creates a culture where people can have an opinion about authoritative figures. This attitude slowly creeps into churches where people lose respect for men and women of God, especially when a story breaks out about a minister. Whether it is a fabricated lie or not, people want to have their opinion and forget men and women of God who are to be shown respect.

Roman 14:4 says "who are you to pass judgment on the servant of another? It is before his master that he stands or falls. And he will be upheld, for the Lord can make him stand."

As Christians, we need to move away from the culture of having negative opinions about men and women of God on social media. Whenever I try and say something negative, the Holy Spirit seals my lips. I cannot open my mouth even if I tried to. I would discipline myself not to say anything bad about a spirit-filled individual; instead I would pray for them.

We allow social media to distract us in church when the Word of God is being preached. People are on social media apps and being distracted. This ought not to be so.

Living a life of intercession
Intercession is the action of intervening on behalf of another in reference to Ezekiel 22:30(ESV) which says: "And I sought for a man among them who should build up the wall and stand in the breach before me for the land that I should not destroy it, but I found none."

If you are reading this book and you have been praying for God to use you, begin with intercession. *Intercessors are not publicly recognized, but they are "dangerous" Christians and a threat to the demonic kingdom.* However, you are recognised in Heaven, angels are assigned to intercessors all the time especially when they begin to pray.

Ask Daniel. "(10) Then behold, a hand touched me and set me trembling on my hands and knees. He said to me, "O Daniel, a man of high esteem, understand the words that I am about to tell you and stand upright, for I have now been sent to you." And when he had spoken this word to me, I stood up trembling. (12) Then he said to me, "Do not be afraid, Daniel, for from the first day that you set your heart on understanding this and on humbling yourself before your God, your words were heard, and I have come in response to your words." - Daniel 10:11-12.(NASB)

When you become an intercessor, you might ask yourself "What should I pray about?" God Himself will give you things to pray about that will blow your mind. Your prayers can save a loved one and can turn a hopeless situation into a comfortable position.

You can avoid national catastrophe because God will show it to you in advance. Moses interceded for the people of Israel who God was angry with, because they began worshipping golden calves. Because I am an intercessor God has often shown me national disasters that will happen to countries. I have seen such things and have prayed about them.

I remember about eight years ago, I told my Dad about a dream and saw a plane flying. Suddenly it started coming down that he turned on the television. Soon after, what I was telling him, it was on the morning news.

Having access to the secrets of God is a mighty thing and must not be taken lightly. It must be treated with the utmost respect. If not, God won't reveal His secrets to us. This is vital for our daily survival due to the evil days we live in.

If you cannot see at all in the spirit, you must pray to God for the power of open eyes and ears.

1 Chronicles 12:32 says, "The children of Issachar, were men that understood the times, knew what Israel ought to do."

The only way to know what time it is spiritually is by understanding times and season, as the sons of Issachar.

We need to tune into the frequency of Heaven. In Joel 2:28- 29 (KJV) it says: *"(28) And it shall come to pass afterward, that I will pour out my spirit upon all flesh; and your sons and your daughters shall prophesy, your old men shall dream dreams, your young men shall see visions. (29) And also upon the servants and upon the handmaids in those days will I pour out my spirit."*

~ CHAPTER 20 ~

ACTIVATION PRAYER

Eyes

Father God, through the blood of Jesus, remove from my spiritual eyes everything that is stopping me from seeing into the supernatural, in Jesus Name I pray, Amen.

Mouth

Father forgive me for anything I have said that did not glorify you. Discipline my tongue with the blood of Jesus and let me declare praises of God. When I pray, let nothing hinder my prayer, in Jesus' Name, Amen.

Ears

Father God, anything blocking me from hearing your voice, I bind and cast it out with the blood of Jesus, so that I can hear your voice clearly. Your word declares that my sheep know my voice and a stranger they would not follow." In Jesus' Name I pray, Amen.

Father God activate my spiritual senses; I want to see you. It would be an honour to experience your power every blessed day. In Jesus' Mighty Name I've prayed, Amen.

BIBLIOGRAPHY

- https://www.biblegateway.com/passage/?search=Psalm+40%3A7-8&version=NKJV
- https://www.biblegateway.com/passage/?search=1+Corinthians+2%3A9&version=NIV
- https://www.openbible.info/topics/cherubim
- https://www.biblegateway.com/verse/en/Malachi%203%3A10
- http://biblehub.com/revelation/3-7.ht
- https://www.bible.com/bible/100/ISA.35.8.nasb
- http://www.cbradiomemories.com/a_word_from_shadow7.htm
- http://www.youtube.com/watch?v=Ze6duhXNz24
- https://www.mormon.org/me/1h9v
- https://bible.org/seriespage/12-apologetics-and-interpretation-fact
- http://bible.knowing-jesus.com/Genesis/28/12
- https://www.biblegateway.com/passage/?search=Psalm+40%3A7-8&version=NKJV
- THE IMPORTANCE OF ENCOUNTERING - Cell Pastors
- Chilton, M. Continuing to invest in our youth. The Charlotte
- http://biblehub.com/greek/1129.htm
- https://www.bible.com/bible/111/2KI.6.8-17
- https://www.biblegateway.com/passage/?search=2%20Kings%206

- http://biblehub.com/hebrews/5-8.htm
- https://www.gotquestions.org/mantle-Bible.html
- https://www.bible.com/bible/111/1KI.19.12-13.niv
- https://www.biblestudytools.com/1-samuel/15-27.html
- https://www.biblestudytools.com/1-samuel/15-27.html
- https://www.gotquestions.org/mantle-Bible.html
- https://www.gotquestions.org/mantle-Bible.html
- http://www.graceauckland.nz/
- https://www.wattpad.com/319155850-back-together-chapter-1
- http://littleinspiration.com/2013/02/10-inspirational-sayings-free-printable.html
- https://www.theepochtimes.com/could-fairies-be-real-alleged-real-life-fairy-photos-fairy-sightings_615895.html
- http://www.floridabuilding.org/fbc/publications/Energy/RIMch1-2_04.pdf
- http://hethathasanear.com/theInheritance.html
- Boney, J. (2016, January 10). Police kill unarmed black men out of fear
- https://soundfaith.com/sermons/116976-covenant-and-mystery?lightbox=sign in

Contacting the Author
Email: vivianneduahodei@gmail.com

Printed in Poland
by Amazon Fulfillment
Poland Sp. z o.o., Wrocław

61397159R00075